'This Squalid Little Room!'

'Lawrence of Arabia'

…the myth, the man and the Hornsea connection

S. F. Taylor

Southfield Writers

In memory of Dr J. E. S. Walker MBE
1934–2015

Contents

Acknowledgements

Firstly, I must thank Stuart Walker, posthumously, for bringing T. E. Lawrence into my life.

My thanks also go to Marvin for his invaluable professional input to the book and his suggestions for improvement; to David for his ever-continuing support; to Thom for yet another brilliant cover design and help with publication; to Maggie for her wonderfully meticulous checking of detail; and to Ian for believing in me and his insistence that I sit down and write, write and write.

I also thank my lovely children for always being there for me: Katie, Joe and Tom.

And latterly I must also thank Philip Neale, Chairman of the T. E. Lawrence Society, for his comments and suggestions!

Sue Fraser Taylor
Trustee and Curator, Hornsea Museum
2010-16

Foreword

In the summer of 2012, Catherine Walker of Hornsea Museum gave me a plastic bag stuffed with hand-written notes, books, letters and files, all in no particular order. The contents had been collected, written and saved by her husband, Dr Stuart Walker, on the subject of Thomas Edward Lawrence. The collection had been accumulated over Dr Walker's many years in Hornsea, both as GP and amateur local historian, and provided the start of what would become my own interest in 'Lawrence of Arabia' – as he was, and is, much better known – and in particular the man who paid visits to Hornsea over the winter of 1934/35.

Catherine and Stuart Walker had been instrumental in setting up Hornsea Museum in 1978, devoting many years to developing it into the thriving community resource that still continues today. Dr Walker had an insatiable appetite for any item of interest or well-known person connected, however tenuously, with the town, and in this instance I believe he had struck gold.

As Curator and Trustee of Hornsea Museum at the time I received this bag of curiosity, as well as having lived in the town for almost twenty years, I confess this was the first I had heard of Lawrence staying here. I knew little of his life beyond a sketchy outline of his time spent in the Middle East fighting alongside the Arabs, and from watching David Lean's 1962 movie *Lawrence of Arabia*, an old video copy of which nestled beneath all the notes and files.

Dr Walker had made it clear that it was his quest to try to understand more about 'one of the most enigmatic men who had ever visited Hornsea'. In his opinion, when Lawrence came to the Sims' house, White Cottage, Eastgate, it was possibly the first time he had fully experienced family life as an adult.

When I began to undertake my own research, I soon realised there are few detailed references to Lawrence's time in Hornsea, either in contemporary accounts or more recent histories. I began by reading Reginald Sims' *The Sayings and Doings of T. E. Lawrence*, which for me brought into focus the personality of the man behind the myth. Unfortunately, the book is not widely available and the price of a second-hand copy is certainly beyond the reach of most pockets.

Numerous definitive and more easily obtainable works consider the life of T. E. Lawrence in great detail, many listed at the end of this book should you wish to consult them. They discuss his early life; his campaigns during the First World War; his years in the RAF; the time he spent at Bridlington; and, of course, his untimely death at the age of just 47. They cover every inch of ground yet often leave more questions than answers for the reader seeking the real Lawrence.

I have tried to encapsulate those aspects of his life that formed the Lawrence of 1934, and to understand the character of the man who briefly graced Hornsea, and the Sims household, with his unique presence. Included in this book are the traits I believe deserve special mention, those pertinent to his nature and temperament during what would prove to be the last year of his life.

I read an unexpurgated version of *The Mint*, finding it a brutally honest portrayal of life as a new recruit in the RAF. Dr Walker was horrified by the 'barrack room' language, but I was riveted by the close description as well as beguiled by Lawrence's motives for enlisting. The year was 1922, and seeking anonymity, he assumed the name of John Hume Ross. After all his achievements, and all he had been through after the war, it was incredible that he should put himself through the mind-numbing, arduous and violent rigours of life at 'The Depot', Uxbridge. Lawrence himself described it as 'a savage place'. The book was eventually published posthumously in 1955, along with an expurgated version for the faint-hearted.

My preliminary reading left me puzzled and intrigued, but most of all eager to know more. Dr Walker's notes were my starting point, and in taking on the task of expanding his research, I hope I have produced something of which he would approve.

S. F. Taylor – 5 September 2017

T. E. Lawrence – a revelation

Wing Commander Reginald Sims first met T. E. Lawrence while he was serving at RAF Catfoss. Of course, Sims was aware of Lawrence's reputation, but he was keen to get to know this national hero on a more personal level. From the visits Lawrence paid to their home, all three members of the Sims family – Reginald, his wife Hilda and son John – derived much pleasure in their different ways. Lawrence delighted young John with his revelations into characters from a children's book, *Heroes of Modern Adventure*. Lawrence called for a pencil and happily corrected details, especially those concerning his own life. 'Lawrence dynamited the Turkish troop trains until it came to be regarded as a little hobby of his,' reported the book. 'Three,' wrote Lawrence underneath. Hardly the 'hobby' described.

Lawrence's visits to Hornsea were not well known at the time, primarily because the Sims respected the privacy they knew their guest craved. Lawrence was constantly pestered by the media and resented any intrusion into his personal life. By 1934 he was tired and world-weary, and beset by depression when he learned that his days in the RAF were numbered.

Over a period of four months in late 1934 and early 1935, while still in the RAF, Lawrence spent several weekends with the Sims family, and on occasion accompanied them on social outings. During that time, they thoroughly enjoyed his company, getting to know the man behind the myth.

Lawrence was, and still is, an enigma. Even within the Walker family opinions were divided. Neither Dr Walker nor any of his classmates at Hymers College, Hull (1940-52) knew that 'Lawrence of Arabia' had stayed in Hornsea. In later years, however, the impression given

1

by Dr Walker's father, an infantry captain in the First World War, was that Lawrence was an unstable, self-opinionated 'loose cannon'. His mother, on the other hand, thought of Lawrence as an 'important and debonair romantic hero'. This dichotomy of opinion was not unusual, and remains today to a certain extent, but either way Lawrence continues to exert a great fascination.

This book will introduce facets of Lawrence's personality that have been subject to the most exacting scrutiny; they have been argued over and have often polarised opinion. Each trait served to shape the man who presented himself to the Sims family in 1934, and all are worth bearing in mind when we consider what he had lived through from his childhood onwards.

I start with the Hornsea connection and follow this with a biographical summary of what I believe are the parts of Lawrence's life most relevant and salient in forming the man and his personality at that time. Sadly, however, it would be within months of his premature death.

Hornsea in the 1930s

Hornsea at this time was trying to attract the 'right sort' of visitors. The town has often projected an air of gentility, looking down upon its neighbouring resorts of Bridlington and Withernsea, and the 1930s was no exception. During the late nineteenth century it had tried to develop as a fashionable sea-bathing resort, when such activity was considered highly beneficial to health. However, it never quite hit the mark. According to the *Victoria County History for East Yorkshire*, the Hornsea of 1873 was described as 'the quaintest mixture of a small country town and a callow sea bathing place'. Having lived here for over twenty years, I can appreciate the sentiment, when

Hornsea hovers between tourist attraction and a residential town that happens to be close to the sea.

By the 1930s, Hornsea had developed into more of a seaside destination for day-trippers, especially with the development of the railway. Travel was cheap and day excursions prolific. 1934 saw 86,000 visitors arrive by rail out of a total annual count of approximately 300,000.

Hornsea in the 1930s

It is also interesting to note that in April 1935 the council imposed a 30mph speed limit on all roads in the town. It is to be hoped that Lawrence, a lover of speed, adhered to the proposed new law when he arrived on his latest motorcycle.

Hornsea has often given the impression that it lags thirty years behind the major cities and towns across the UK, and the 1930s exemplifies this perception. The first telephone kiosks arrived in August 1930, twenty-seven years after their inception in London; even the streetlights continued to be powered by gas. Perhaps this explains why Lawrence warmed to the town; perhaps, too, Hornsea came as close to the ideal of Clouds Hill, the Dorset cottage he had renovated for his retirement, as he could find while stationed at Catfoss.

Lawrence and the Hornsea Connection

Lawrence spent the last sixteen weeks of his RAF service on the east coast of Yorkshire, mainly in Bridlington. Little of substance was recorded of his visits to Hornsea. Dr Walker, however, did manage to acquire some snippets of colloquial knowledge from the more elderly among his patients as well as from his colleagues. As a newly qualified GP, Dr Walker started his career at Ivy Lodge, Eastgate – a Georgian house which, apart from a decade c.1880-90, served as a doctor's residence and surgery from 1830 to 1962. It became known in Hornsea that Dr Walker had an interest in local history, and he made notes of all the varied facts and pieces of information that came his way, gathering as much as he could for future reference.

From the start of the National Health Service in 1948, the dispenser and manageress at Ivy Lodge was Miss Olive Russell. She talked frequently about 'Wing Co. Sims' and his family, who lived next door at White Cottage, Number 3, Eastgate, and who were visited several times by 'Lawrence of Arabia', shortly before his death in a motorcycle accident. Over time, Dr Walker grew convinced of the veracity of Miss Russell's information, finding much of it confirmed by the facts he later unearthed from other locals, and by all that he had read.

So who was the man welcomed by the Sims into their home in 1934, and how did he come across to this Hornsea family?

Flight Lieutenant Reginald G. Sims was then based at RAF Catfoss, six miles west of Hornsea, in command of the Bridlington detachment. Reginald, his wife Hilda, son John and dog Chummy lived at White Cottage, Hornsea, which soon became something of a local landmark when it became known that Aircraftman 1st Class T. E. Shaw, the famous 'Lawrence of Arabia', had spent many evenings and weekends there during his last four months in the RAF.

Sims' first meeting with Lawrence had an inauspicious start, however. Of the day he first asked Lawrence to Hornsea for lunch, Sims recalled: 'a pair of the bluest, most flashing eyes I had ever seen blazed forth, while a vast forehead, equal in size to the terrific chin beneath, simply radiated scorn and hate at me.'

Reginald G. Sims, 1931

Plagued by the press since his involvement in the Arab Revolt during the First World War, Lawrence at first believed Sims was just another despised journalist. But when Sims corrected him, Lawrence realised his mistake and apologised.

The subsequent lunch saw the beginning of a close friendship and frequent visits to the White Cottage. Reginald ascertained that Lawrence did not drive cars, noting later that, unlike a speeding motorcycle: '…a car was of too stable an equilibrium for him to enjoy driving'.

One subsequent weekend, the weather was wild and stormy and Lawrence stayed over for the night. He and the Sims stayed up until 1.45am, by the fireside, where Lawrence talked and the family listened with rapt concentration: 'We sat listening entranced to that very quiet, clear voice, utterly dominated by the terrific charm that surrounded him.'

Reginald remarked more than once on Lawrence's voice and diction: 'Each word he used was the perfect one selected by a Master Craftsman of language'.

It is interesting to note this use of the term 'Master Craftsman', which could be applied to many aspects of Lawrence's life, from the writing and construction of his books, to his work on his cottage at Clouds Hill, to his involvement with boats and machinery. He was nothing if not meticulous in all he undertook. His writing, too, has a beauty of poetry in his descriptions. At Cadet College at RAF Cranwell, he wrote of a lone autumn-evening walk at the camp: 'By the yard gate the ragged leaves of a plane-tree lay upturned, so ashy pale on the black grass edging the road that they gathered the moonlight: and at first I thought them torn pages from a note-book.'

Lawrence did not want to impose upon the Sims family, but once persuaded to stay overnight, he never objected again. It is believed that Lawrence slept in a small upstairs bedroom at the back of White Cottage – subsequently designated by the family 'Aurens Room', after the Arab pronunciation of Lawrence. Hanging on the wall was a photograph of the bronze bust sculpted in 1919 by Derwent Wood, when Lawrence was attending the Paris Peace Conference (although the sitter did not much care for it, it is now at the Imperial

War Museum, with a cast at the Tate). And it was in this room, two years after Lawrence's death, that Reginald Sims compiled his own book: *The Sayings and Doings of T. E. Lawrence.*

The Sims also had an area in the sitting room where they kept several gifts from Lawrence, including one folio book, remembered by their Hornsea visitors, which contained full-length colour portraits of Lawrence's Arab colleagues during the Arab Revolt.

White Cottage, Eastgate, Hornsea

Lawrence also joined the Sims on several visits to orchestral concerts in Hull, as well as to places of interest like Beverley Minster. Their home may perhaps have offered some respite from his tormented state of mind at that time. Viewing photographs of Clouds Hill, taken by Walton Adams in April 1935, after Lawrence had restored the cottage, and comparing them with the layout of the sitting room in White Cottage, it is easy to imagine why Lawrence felt so much at home there.

In one of his last letters, written from Clouds Hill, he wrote of 'getting used to an empty life' after leaving the RAF. There was an air of sadness about the man whose deeds were so great, who had tried

7

so hard to shun the fame and notoriety that accompanied them, and who had struggled to cope with the disappointing aftermath of the Arab Revolt. He had lived through so much, yet had gained little satisfaction from all he had striven to achieve.

What, of course, was never mentioned, and the Sims family probably never knew, was that while stationed in the East Riding, Lawrence made six or seven trips to Perth, Edinburgh, London and Aberdeen for 'disciplines' of twelve strokes of the birch, administered by John Bruce. These will be discussed later, along with suggestions as to why he was compelled to undertake such 'punishments'.

Introducing Lawrence into their social circle would have brought great kudos to the Sims family, but they kept his visits to themselves and their discretion was appreciated. With their great respect for Lawrence, they recognised that he was essentially a private and vulnerable man who shunned publicity; they felt the need to shelter him from prying eyes. Reginald also gained the impression that Lawrence did not like to be touched or even brushed against. The two had shaken hands at their initial meeting, but no further contact was ever forthcoming.

That said, the Sims were privileged to get to know the man better than most during the last months of his life. On one occasion Lawrence voiced his approval of the new and innovative materials then coming into general use in the domestic setting: steel, Bakelite and coloured glass rather than painted woodwork and coloured wallpaper. (He had lined one room at Clouds Hill with asbestos and steel to insulate it from the extremes of heat and cold.)

'In a hundred years from now, no-one would think of sitting in a squalid little room like this,' he reportedly told the family. Reginald Sims must have raised an eyebrow at the observation: it was said 'in our own drawing room and before our very faces, if you please,' he later noted. But he also remarked that Lawrence accompanied it with a serious smile and an 'impish twinkle in his eye'. Lawrence was nothing if not brutally honest in his remarks, yet he did not give offense.

When Reginald took it upon himself to record his memories of Lawrence, he wrote of the recollections he had gleaned from other colleagues and friends of Lawrence. The Sayings & Doings of T. E. Lawrence was eventually published by Reginald's son John in 1994. The book mentions Lawrence's habit of smoking one or two cigarettes a year: 'As T. E. did not stay with us during either Christmas or Easter leave, we were not able to offer him the one cigarette which he told us he always smoked on those occasions; he smoked only one cigarette, not for the pleasure of doing so but to feel happy that he was not obsessed in any way by the habit of smoking.'

This was just one of many instances of Lawrence's obsession with abstinence and supreme self-control: 'We had offered him beer and wine at his first visit, but he refused anything to drink but water. He approved the taste of the local water supplied to Hornsea. He posed as a good judge of that fluid and could hazard a fairly accurate guess as to the origin of any he drank – tap, well, river – and in some cases the geographical position of the source of supply.'

Hornsea tap water by that time came from boreholes in the chalk via Hull Corporation, and was stored in the large white-painted concrete tank, currently standing on the edge of Hornsea Golf Course at Seats Hill, a mile south of the town.

Sims noted conversations with Lawrence where he would give them 'in brilliant cameos, sketches of kings, beggars, celebrities, underdogs, artists, murderers and friends whom he had met.' Sims was fascinated by Lawrence, and obviously was thrilled to have him as a guest in his home, but he never once abused what he felt was an honour, nor used it for personal advantage.

Hornsea Water Tower

A talented amateur photographer, Sims also took a series of portrait photographs of Lawrence at White Cottage, thoughtful and studious images that would be among the last ever taken.

In November 2007, Dr Walker received a letter from Timothy French, a Hornsea boy who knew John Sims, accompanied by selected pages from *T. E. Lawrence by His Friends*, published in 1954 by Lawrence's younger brother Arnold. Within these pages, Reginald recalls the incident involving *Heroes of Modern Adventure* – when Lawrence wrote in the margins of the book, correcting perceived inaccuracies in the text – and adds that the book had been loaned to John by a friend.

That friend was Alan Brown, who confirmed the truth of this story and who, despite repeated requests, never saw his book again. French had it on good authority that 'there was no dinner party of thanks for the "lovable" little boy and no book return!' as recorded in *Lawrence by His Friends*. French also wrote that 'many years later John admitted that when he was a bit hard up, he sold a number of items of interest concerning Lawrence and the book was one of them'.

On John Sims' marriage in 1957, he and his wife received a gift from Lawrence's mother, Sarah – a silver chalice brought back from Urfa by her son. John recalled that Mrs Lawrence 'thought I would like to have something to remind me of "my friendship with Ned".'

During his time at White Cottage, Lawrence also became friendly with Peter Barugh, a Hornsea man who kept a yacht in Bridlington Harbour. When Lawrence came through to Hornsea on his motorbike, Peter often received a lift home. 'The most hair-raising rides of my life', Peter is known to have described these journeys. This is hardly surprising given that speed was Lawrence's drug of choice. He once wrote that 'at 80 [mph] or so, I feel the earth moulding herself under me...I could write pages on the lustfulness of moving swiftly'. (Henry Williamson, *Genius of Friendship*)

It was probably on the recommendation of Reginald Sims that Lawrence had his motorcycle, 'George VII', serviced at Seaton Garage, two miles west of Hornsea. Stanley Burrows of Skirlaugh (d. 2003) was a most obliging motor mechanic and remembered carrying out the service and meeting Lawrence more than once. Friends including George Bernard Shaw and his wife Charlotte had sometimes paid for Lawrence's motorbikes; Charlotte, in particular, knew that speed was essential to Lawrence, vital to his life and well-being. It is interesting to note that at the time of his death, Lawrence had just ordered 'George VIII'.

AC1 Shaw on one of his Brough Superior motorcycles

Special modifications were made to his motorcycles, which made them difficult for anyone else to ride. Lawrence, whose character displayed elements of paranoia, had his controls set on the opposite side to conventional models to make his bikes difficult to steal. If one were to be stolen, it would also then be quite easy to prove who it belonged to.

Sadly there are no more reports of Lawrence's time in Hornsea, certainly none in the detail revealed by Reginald Sims.
Yet, through all I have read, including Reginald's own words, my claim now is that the Sims family welcomed one of the most mystifying and inspirational men of the twentieth century.

The following potted biography will highlight Lawrence's achievements, disappointments and friendships, hopefully giving an insight into his state of mind during his last days with the RAF and at Hornsea. His life has been subject to endless scrutiny, and some of his achievements questioned, but nothing detracts from the fascination he still exerts today. The family at White Cottage – Reginald, Hilda, John and Chummy the dog – were privileged to get to know Lawrence on a personal level and at a period of his life devoted more to reflection and resignation than to action, and no-one realised more than Reginald what an honour it was to listen to all that Lawrence had to say.

The Sayings and Doings of T. E. Lawrence may have been written two years after Lawrence's death, and some details may have become blurred or been misinterpreted, but this does not detract from the love and admiration that suffuses every page.

Yet the question that remains is this: who was the real T. E. Lawrence, and how much of that man can be found in the persona of the fabled 'Lawrence of Arabia' who visited Hornsea?

Family Life – hating the sin but loving the sinner

From the little that Lawrence wrote about his early life, it soon becomes obvious that his childhood was far from easy. His grandfather, Sir William Chapman, was an Anglo-Irish baronet from County Meath, whose son, Thomas Robert Tighe Chapman, married Edith Hamilton Boyd on 24 July 1873. The couple subsequently had four daughters, and Thomas would no doubt have been disappointed that he had no son. Thomas ran his estate, enjoying the traditional pursuits of fishing, shooting and sailing. He was a man of considerable passion, ultimately not reciprocated by his wife Edith. Upon becoming better acquainted with the girls' Scottish governess, Sarah Junner, he realised his mistake. Where Edith had turned out to be 'a ferocious spouse who considered any form of amusement to be a sin', Sarah proved far more receptive to him. Edith was unreasonably strict and so fanatically religious that she was nicknamed in Dublin circles 'The Holy Viper'.

Thomas completely abandoned his home, wife and four daughters to sail to England with the small, neat, pretty Sarah, at the same time changing the family name to Lawrence. Leaving behind an honourable and affluent lifestyle, Thomas's income was reduced to just £300 a year. He had to give up all but the simplest country pursuits, abandoning ocean racing, selling his sporting guns and substituting a bicycle for his hunter.

Thomas and Sarah had five sons but never married. The stigma of illegitimacy cannot be under-estimated at this time, and with each pregnancy Sarah ensured that the family moved to a new location, lest the truth be discovered.

Sarah Lawrence at Langley Lodge, Fawley, Southampton c.1895. L to R ~ Thomas, William, Frank, Robert (Bodleian Library)

The eldest son, Montagu Robert, known in the family as Bob, was born in Dublin in December 1885. Always correct, polite and kind, he was an academic who became a missionary in China, where his mother joined him in her later years.

The second son, Thomas Edward, known as Ned within the family, but in later life more famously as 'Lawrence of Arabia', was born at Tremadog in north Wales on 16 August 1888. He would be the most resourceful, self-reliant and resolute member of the family.

The third son, William George, was born in Kirkcudbright (Scotland) in 1889. He was a handsome boy whose life would be cut short when he was killed in action in October 1915.

After a short stay in the Isle of Man, the family next moved to Dinard on the Breton coast, then to St Helier in Jersey, ensuring British nationality for the fourth son, Frank Helier, born in February 1893. Sadly, Frank would also be killed in action, in May 1915, during the battle of Aubers Ridge.

The family's final move was to Oxford, where Arnold Walter was born in 1900. He became an archaeologist and art historian, and later a professor of archaeology.

Herself born out of wedlock, Sarah felt enormous guilt that this taint was also borne by her sons. To atone for her actions, she took comfort from a leading Evangelical churchman, Canon Alfred Christopher, who preached that 'God hates the sin, but loves the sinner', especially one that shows repentance. Sarah, too, became a strict disciplinarian and Evangelical Christian, who believed that children inherit the sins of their parents.

If Lawrence was disobedient or too wilful, he received severe beatings from his mother, and this eventually took its toll upon their relationship. He was never a man to reveal his feelings, but at the age of 39, he admitted to Charlotte Shaw, with whom he developed a rare, close personal relationship: 'I have a terror of her [Sarah] knowing anything about my feelings, or convictions, or way of life.'

In effect, he tried to cut himself off from such emotions. This may also have prompted his dislike of physical contact.

Lawrence was aged around 10 when he became aware that he was illegitimate. Despite his father's aristocratic background, the irregularity of his parents' relationship meant the family's position in society would always be denied. Lawrence knew he had not been born with a silver spoon in his mouth. His illegitimacy significantly influenced his behaviour over the years and would have exerted a considerable impact on his marriage prospects, should he ever have wished to wed.

School Years – 'an irrelevant and time-wasting nuisance'

Lawrence attended the City of Oxford High School for Boys, where he was a prodigious reader, capable of devouring three books a day. He was not afraid of hardship or exertion; in fact, he reveled in testing his endurance. His mother wished everyone to believe that his schooldays were the happiest time of his life, but Lawrence claimed this was far from the case. He confirmed to his biographer, Basil Liddell Hart, that 'they were miserable sweated years of unwilling work', and an 'irrelevant and time-wasting nuisance'. He was far happier with the freedom brought by university: 'Oxford, after it [school], so noble a freedom'.

Lawrence was a small man – only 5ft 5½ inches tall (although his height was sympathetically recorded as 5ft 6 inches to pass his RAF medical). His stature may be related to a leg broken after an argument with a boy at school, or perhaps to a dose of mumps contacted during puberty. His leg was weakened by the fracture and he started to use a bicycle more often. As a teenager, he cycled to the south of France to visit castles and take brass rubbings, and aged 17, he slipped away from home and rode to Cornwall, where he enlisted in the Royal Artillery. His father collected him three weeks later, having bought him out of the army, and took him home.

To avoid domestic disruption, and to accommodate Lawrence's eccentric sleeping hours, his father then built him a small house in the back garden. This allowed him to study undisturbed, and ultimately he gained a place at Jesus College, Oxford, where he graduated with First Class Honours in History.

University Life – and the walk of a thousand miles, 1907-10

Lawrence was a highly intelligent man with quick responses. He also developed an extremely complex and somewhat disturbed mind with masochistic tendencies, as will be expanded upon later.

He was multi-lingual too. He learned Arabic as an undergraduate so he could converse with the locals when he toured the Middle East, collecting material for his thesis on the architecture of the Crusader castles. A strenuous regime of preparation included long cycle rides and cross-country treks, and he spent hours perfecting his marksmanship on the range, using a pistol in either hand. He also went for days without food, and at least once a week would sit through a college dinner without eating a thing. He had little interest in sport but, enjoying his eccentricity, he pushed himself physically to extremes. In 1908 he joined the Oxford University Officer Training Corps, widely considered as rigorous as Sandhurst.

Back at university, a great student friend was an Anglo-American undergraduate, Vivian Richards. Both men were absorbed by the Arts and Crafts Movement and undertook research into its founder, William Morris. They even planned to build a Utopian house together in Epping Forest – revealing an interest in the aesthetic and practical application of materials that stayed with Lawrence throughout his life. He was very adept with his hands and could be very innovative.

Lawrence aged 22 with his brothers, 1910
L to R ~ Thomas, Will, Arnold, Bob and Frank.

The two men grew extremely close in the course of this project, and in 1969 Richards sought to put the record straight. For him, he admitted, it was love at first sight; on Lawrence's part, however, the affection was 'uncomfortably and irritatingly, pure'. Richards believed that Lawrence was 'unaware of sex' at the time –.evidence once more of a rejection of the physical side of a relationship, male or female.

Lawrence's life has been scrutinised in every last detail with regards to his alleged homosexuality. Yet he remains the ultimate enigma. As in every other facet of his character, nothing has ever been proved. While not overtly homosexual, some aspects of his behaviour could easily lead to that assumption. Nor did he have a close relationship with any of the young ladies of his generation. The nearest he came to revealing his innermost sentiments to a member of the opposite sex was with Charlotte Shaw.

Post University – travel and pre-war preparation

In 1911, at the age of 23, Lawrence became a practising archaeologist in the Middle East. He took part in a British Museum expedition to Mesopotamia, returning fluent in many different dialects of Arabic. He used his strong diplomatic and persuasive powers to settle disharmony among the men and obtained from them more work than was customary on digs. He was also working on a War Office survey, travelling through Syria and amending and upgrading maps. This built upon his previous knowledge and experience of the Arab world and would prove extremely useful during the Arab Revolt three years later.

In January 1914, seven months before the outbreak of the First World War, Lawrence and fellow archaeologist Leonard Woolley were co-opted by the British Army to undertake a survey of the Negev Desert. The survey was supposedly for archaeological purposes, but in reality, as Lawrence reported to his mother, it was to spy on Turkish defences in southern Palestine, approximately 100 miles from the Suez Canal. The canal was always a priority for the British, allowing ships travelling to India to avoid circumnavigating Africa. When war broke out that August, Lawrence and Woolley were back in England. They were ordered to finish their report quickly, at the same time making the survey appear solely archaeological.

1914-1918 – Lawrence and the Arab Revolt

Lawrence remained in the War Office until late 1914, when Lord Kitchener, Secretary of State for War, sent him to Egypt to work with the Military Intelligence Service. Lawrence played a major role in the Arab Revolt against the Turks; in 1916 he received permission to strike inland and established a relationship with Faisal ibn Hussein, the third son of the instigator of the uprising, Grand Sharif Hussein bin Ali. It was feared that the Arabs were close to supporting the Germans, causing great consternation to a British government in turmoil over the introduction of conscription. In March 1916, the Military Service Act was passed allowing conscription of single men between the ages of 18 and 41, and in May it was extended to cover married men of the same age. However, the Act was immensely unpopular, with over 200,000 people protesting in Trafalgar Square in April 1916.

In consequence the British had formulated no plan of action to deal with the developing Arab crisis. In 1915, the Ottoman Turks had allied with Germany, threatening the Suez Canal, Britain's lifeline to the Empire. The Ottoman Empire had ruled the Middle East for centuries, and the French also had claims on the region. Lawrence was passionately opposed to any French presence, hoping to oust the Ottomans and 'biff the French out of all hope of Syria'.

This extreme antipathy to the French – irrefutable from his own words and from biographical accounts – is hard to explain. Lawrence loved French history, architecture and literature. Perhaps it stemmed more from the British and French struggle for dominance in the region, as well as his absolute pro-Arab stance.

Lawrence in Arab dress with the gold dagger
made for him in Mecca, 1917

East Riding men who had originally enlisted as troopers in the East Riding Yeomanry, were transferred to the region to join the Imperial Camel Corps, and one of their tasks was to blow up sections of the Hejaz Railway. This 700-mile line running from Medina to Istanbul was essential to the Turks for transporting supplies and reinforcements. With great fervour and the swift deployment of slender resources, Lawrence developed into a sound tactician and intrepid guerilla fighter, with a vision of what the Arabs might achieve in their quest for nationhood. He planned and organised the destruction of crucial sections of track when military trains were passing north to Syria.

However, the resulting massacre of the Turks on 27 March 1917 haunted Lawrence for years to come. Acts of violence did not sit comfortably with him: 'Ours should be a war of detachment. We were to contain the enemy by the silent threat of a vast unknown desert, not disclosing ourselves till we attacked...and develop a habit of never engaging the enemy.'

The wreckage of the train and the dead bodies were plundered, and the injured left to die without medics to treat them. Success was exhilarating to the Arabs, but Lawrence was wracked with guilt: 'I'm not going to last out this game much longer...this killing and killing of Turks is horrible.'

However, the Arabs continued to fight, and while sabotaging other sections of railway near the Syrian town of Deraa, Lawrence was taken prisoner on 20 November 1917. He describes his capture and subsequent torture and rape in *Seven Pillars of Wisdom*, and again in his post-war letters. Something profound clearly occurred at Deraa, but the episode continues to provoke much speculation. Historians and biographers argue over the veracity of Lawrence's account, some even doubting that the events described took place at all. Whatever the truth of the matter, the incident undoubtedly had an enormous effect on Lawrence's behaviour in the years that followed, inflicting psychological scars that would never really heal.

The Aftermath of War

Lawrence eventually left the army with the rank of colonel. It is possible that Field Marshal Allenby, commander of the Egyptian

Expeditionary Force gave Lawrence the necessary 'crown and pips' so he could enjoy a first-class compartment on the long, slow rail trip back to the UK, when Allenby knew the world's press would be waiting. The spectre of fame haunted Lawrence for the rest of his life, and nothing he could do would diminish public interest in him, be they for or against 'Lawrence of Arabia'.

During his time with the Arabs, Lawrence had promised them self-government, free from outside interference, and in 1919 he and Faisal went to the Paris Peace Conference to argue the Arab case and secure an independent state. Sadly, he soon realised that the British government, together with France and the League of Nations, would renege on his assurances.

Faisal ibn Hussein
at the time of the Paris Peace Conference, 1919

Lawrence felt used and accused the British government of wasting the contacts he had worked so hard to establish. He was proud of his success in Arabia, of adapting to the Arab way of life, and of coping with severe deprivation in pursuing the goals he had set for himself, but he would always remain disillusioned at his betrayal.

In 1921 Lawrence was recruited into the Colonial Office as British Adviser on Arab Affairs, but by then he was mentally and physically exhausted, believing that he had failed in all he set out to do. Despite the efforts of Winston Churchill, he resigned his post and took the opportunity to edit his writings on his experiences as a British soldier from 1916 to 1918, producing an autobiographical account of fighting with rebel forces during the Arab conflict against the Ottoman Turks in the work that later became *Seven Pillars of Wisdom*.

Personality and Friendships – perversion and pain

Lawrence was an observant, creative and practical man. His instinctive judgements served him well throughout his time in Syria. Working with the Arabs and their leaders, he learned quickly who could trust and who he could work with, choosing for example Faisal ibn Hussein in preference to Faisal's brothers.

Despite his intellectual capacity and academic distinction at Oxford, Lawrence had never wanted the life of a don. His admiration for fine craftsmanship is shown by his lifelong appreciation of the works of men like William Morris. During his second stint in the RAF he wrote: 'Those we regard as our natural aristocracy show three generations of artisan forebears by their mere grip of the tool-handle.' He also believed that: 'the Air Ministry recognises a rightness in our worship of the technical engineer'.

He cared nothing for possessions and felt that most were unnecessary encumbrances. After experiencing high office, he was content to live on the basic necessities of life, and nowhere was this better illustrated than in his love of Clouds Hill, the Dorset cottage he prepared and developed for his retirement.

In later years, Lawrence donated much of the royalties from his writings to charities such as the RAF Benevolent Fund and other needy causes, and this sometimes left him in a very precarious financial state.

Lawrence was considered a good and reliable friend and was generally well liked by those closest to him. From his earliest undergraduate years, he was in touch with many leading politicians, philosophers and writers such as George Bernard Shaw, Charlotte Shaw (who became his closest confidante and a regular correspondent), Winston Churchill, Lady Astor, Robert Graves and Noel Coward. Throughout his life Lawrence was a prolific writer and often sent several letters a day.

Upon retirement, when Lawrence's income would be considerably reduced, Reginald Sims ventured that he would need to cut down: 'The suggestion that printed cards be obtained, telling all and sundry that he would pare his correspondence to the minimum in future was very favourably received.'

Thus, a prized Sims' possession was later a postcard addressed to 'The Sims Family and Dog', and printed as follows: 'To tell you that in future I shall write very few letters. T. E. S.'

One of several instances in which I detect a quiet sense of humour.

Although his relationships with women were purely platonic, in his friendships with Nancy, Lady Astor and Charlotte Shaw he showed another side to his personality. His letters were intellectual, engaging, even playful, and his words reveal a man comfortable with his own thoughts, ideas and opinions. He wrote to Nancy Astor on 22 July 1929: 'Dear Lady Astor, I do not know when, or with whom, I have ever maintained for so long a hot correspondence. Clearly we are soul mates.'

Charlotte Shaw

Strangely, Lawrence found it easy to open up emotionally to Charlotte Shaw, despite a difference of over thirty years in age. Their letters reveal respect, trust and genuine affection, as well as shared interests in the arts and literature, showing his feelings in a way he never did with his mother. Very possibly, he found in Charlotte the mother he had always craved.

Charlotte Shaw, wife of George Bernard Shaw

Lawrence began writing to Charlotte in 1923, soon after joining the RAF, at a time when he was trying to escape the confines of fame. He admitted that: 'I've not written letters of this sort to anyone else, since I was born...I never have to be conscious of an audience in writing to you.'

John Bruce

Lawrence's relationship with John Bruce was a bizarre aspect of his life, despite their shared experience of service in the Tank Corps and the RAF. Developed more from need than from any intimacy or affection, I feel the relationship merits special attention because of its connotations.

Throughout much of his life, Lawrence derived a perverse fulfillment from enduring hardship. Although he successfully overcame the fatigue and deprivation he experienced after the beatings and alleged rape inflicted by Turkish soldiers at Deraa in 1917, these appear to have left him with a masochistic streak. To conquer his frequent bouts of depression, he would engineer a 'fix of adrenalin' to lift him out of it, either through the exhilaration of speed, or by proving to himself that he could tolerate extreme physical pain. Hence the need for Bruce's services.

Lawrence first met Bruce in early 1922 at the Mayfair flat of a Mr Murray, a friend of Bruce's doctor, and shortly afterwards Lawrence approached the young man with a very unusual job offer. Lawrence explained that he wanted someone young, strong and alert, who could be trusted with highly confidential personal matters, and who would do what he was told without question. He needed to be able to look after himself and possibly others too.

'Everything will be legal and above board,' Lawrence reassured Bruce, going on to explain that he was currently in financial trouble and that he might have to submit to 'unpleasant things' with which he would need assistance. Looking Lawrence in the eye, Bruce told him he did not think he was the man for the job. But after sleeping on it, and phoning his father, who said 'you can always back out if you wish', Bruce accepted and was put on a retainer of £3 a week for three months.

In the strictest confidence, Lawrence explained that he had expected to benefit from his father's estate when Thomas died in 1919, but instead it went to an uncle described by him as 'The Old Man'. The 'Old Man' was unhappy that Lawrence had left the Foreign Office, accusing him of insulting Winston Churchill and others in high places. In short, Lawrence had brought the family name into disrepute, and unless he agreed to his uncle's demands, the details of his birth would be exposed. 'He called me a bastard and meant it,' Lawrence kept repeating. 'How he must hate us for my father's sins.'

Lawrence still found it hard to come to terms with the knowledge that his father and mother had never married and that he and his brothers were illegitimate.

According to Lawrence, a letter sent by 'The Old Man' demanded that he (Lawrence) receive twelve strokes of the birch and Bruce was asked to administer the punishment. Needless to say, Bruce required considerable persuasion before he agreed to the job. Nevertheless, he carried it out, followed by a further twelve strokes on the buttocks before the 'Old Man' was satisfied. Only then was the punishment judged adequate and Bruce was paid for his services.

On 19 July 1924, Lawrence wrote to Charlotte Shaw: 'Bruce (a Scotsman, inarticulate, excessively uncomfortable) comes to Clouds Hill quite often on Sundays; will enter only if I am alone, glares and glowers at me until I put some Beethoven on the gramophone, and then sits solid with a heroic aura of solidarity round him; with myself a squashed door man of fossilized bones between two layers.'

John Bruce in 1923

Given the secretive and bizarre nature of their activities, and Lawrence's reliance on their relationship, John Bruce promised Charlotte Shaw and Lawrence's solicitor that he would not publish his memoirs until after Sarah Lawrence's death. By then, November 1959, he had written a short account of his relationship with Lawrence, but he did not publish until he became seriously ill and needed the money. At the time of their connection, Lawrence had also become godfather to Bruce's son, as well as making an allowance to Mrs Bruce from his RAF pay.

The RAF – a lifelong passion

After lobbying his contacts in high places to help him enlist as a private in the Royal Air Force – created in April 1918 through the amalgamation of the Royal Flying Corps. and the Royal Naval Air Service – Lawrence finally joined up in August 1922. Then aged 34, he gave his name as John Hume Ross and undertook basic training at Uxbridge. Unfortunately, when posted to the RAF School of Photography in Farnborough, his real identity was revealed to the press by one of the officers. He became headline news in the *Daily Express* on 27 December 1922, causing embarrassment to the authorities and eventually leading to his dismissal from the service.

Devastated, Lawrence changed his name to T. E. Shaw, probably in deference to George Bernard and Charlotte Shaw, and in 1923 he joined the Royal Tank Corps. Yet he was unhappy with this state of affairs; the RAF was his passion, and as a determined character, he continued to use his connections to try to engineer a return.

By May 1924 Lawrence had earned a reputation as a non-fiction author, and the Air Ministry suggested he would be the ideal person to write the history of the RAF. He went up to London and was told that, if he agreed, the Ministry might accept his re-enlistment as an RAF officer on a three-year term. He declined the offer and returned instead to Bovington Camp in Dorset, where he became a storeman, a job that gave him ample time to read through the proofs of *Seven Pillars of Wisdom*.

Still, Lawrence remained well connected. On his birthday on 16 August 1924, he was visited by Air Vice-Marshal Sir John Salmond and his wife, who insisted on taking him out for dinner. Lawrence wrote again to Air Chief Marshal Trenchard but once more he was rejected. He was in limbo, depressed and very disturbed. In a letter to his literary adviser Edward Garnett, he wrote of suicide, and raised the subject again during one of his visits to Trenchard. 'All right,' replied Trenchard, refusing to take the threat seriously, 'but please go into the garden. I don't want my carpets ruined.'

Only when he met novelist and politician John Buchan, 1st Baron Tweedsmuir, who put his plight to Prime Minister Stanley Baldwin, did Lawrence obtain his much-coveted transfer back to the RAF. Elated, he proudly recorded that returning to Bovington Camp he reached 108mph on his Brough Superior motorcycle, one of the series he named 'Boanerges', from the Hebrew for 'sons of thunder', and also successively named and numbered 'George I' through to 'George VIII'.

On 19 August 1925, Lawrence left the army and his nightmare months in the Tank Corps and reported for his medical at RAF West Drayton as Aircraftman T. E. Shaw. He was posted first to Uxbridge, then to the Cadet College at RAF Cranwell. The final chapter of *The Mint* records his time at Cranwell; after only two days he knew that he 'had found a home'. In his free time he found exhilaration in riding 'Boanerges', kept in a garage hut at the camp, speeding along the local roads as fast and as often as he could.

In December 1926 Lawrence was posted to India, but while serving on the Afghan frontier he was suspected of involvement in secret service activities. The Afghan government issued an order for his arrest, and this probably prompted his recall from India two years later.

On his return Lawrence continued to ride his motorbike. On occasion he would take it and 'hurl it at top speed through these unfit roads for hour after hour. My nerves are jaded and gone – near dead, so that nothing less than hours of voluntary danger will prick them into life.'

By now 41 years old, Lawrence was showing signs of middle age. He had put on weight and was slowing down; his sight and hearing were not as keen as they were and he felt the cold. His mind began to turn towards a more settled life – just what was offered by his next posting to RAF Cattewater, near Plymouth. In a complete departure from anything he had done before, he was instrumental in the development of the fast ocean-going Class 200 Seaplane, which would also serve as an air-sea rescue launch.

Lawrence also formed part of the team that serviced the British entries in the annual 27-mile Schneider Trophy race around the Isle of Wight. Interestingly, the last-ever race, held in 1931, was won by Reginald J. Mitchell's Supermarine S6B. And it was Mitchell who would subsequently design the first Spitfire, flown by Captain Joseph 'Mutt' Summers, a Hornsea man and noted test pilot for Supermarine and Vickers.

Clouds Hill – planning for retirement

Clouds Hill is the Dorset cottage first rented by Lawrence in 1923, then purchased by him in 1925 using money raised through the sale of his prized gold-shafted Arab dagger. Situated little more than a mile north of Bovington Camp, the cottage offered a convenient refuge where Lawrence could slip away to write and carry out renovations. He used it 'to escape the animal reek here which keeps me awake at night with the horror that mankind should be like it.'

Clouds Hill was a very basic dwelling: 'In my cottage there is no food and no bed,' wrote Lawrence. 'At nightfall there is a flea bag, and I lay on the preferred patch of floor in either room. The ground floor room is for books and the (up) stair room is for music – gramophone and records. There are 5 acres of rhododendrons and fires every evening from their sticks.'

Another sleeping bag was kept for visitors, who were allowed to choose where they placed it.

Clouds Hill after its 1934 refurbishment

George Bernard Shaw visited Clouds Hill in 1924. He helped Lawrence to re-draft *Seven Pillars of Wisdom*, and was a man in whom Lawrence placed a great deal of trust. 'He came in snuffing the air and taking stock of everything like a sergeant-major,' wrote Lawrence. 'I really think he liked it.'

Lawrence spent his summer leave in 1933 at Clouds Hill, replacing the floor and installing piped water, a boiler, a bath and shelving for his books in preparation for retirement. By the time he left the RAF, he had refurbished Clouds Hill to the condition that can still be viewed today, courtesy of the National Trust, which took over the conservation and upkeep of the cottage and now runs it as a museum and visitor attraction.

T. E. Shaw in Bridlington

A sundial on the South Promenade in Bridlington, erected as a memorial to T. E. Lawrence, indicates that as Aircraftman Shaw he was in Bridlington as early as 1929. No details of this visit can be traced but it may have been a short stop while sailing a launch en route to another RAF coastal establishment.

In the spring of 1932 Captain Kelly Rogers and crew Mr Kinnard, Mr Hotham and AC Shaw were delivering a seaplane tender from RAF Calshot on Southampton Water to RAF Donibristle, Fife. En route, they stayed in Bridlington, spending a Saturday night at Mrs Gibson's boarding house at Number 10, Esplanade. In late June, Shaw was back again, for about six weeks this time; after delivering two more launches, he stayed with Mrs Gibson while overseeing their fitting out.

His final RAF posting, from 15 November 1934 to 26 February 1935, was at 1140 Marine Unit, Bridlington – a detachment of the Armament and Weapons Training Unit at RAF Catfoss. Lawrence was billeted with a small detachment at the Ozone Hotel at the junction of West Street and The Crescent. Here, he spent much of his spare time in his bedroom, reading and taking advantage of a borrowed typewriter. His handwriting was not particularly legible and he was planning to submit some work for literary appraisal.

Planes from RAF Catfoss would drop 8-pound metal canisters as bombs on target boats towed from Bridlington Bay to an area east of the cliff-top target range at Skipsea. At AC Shaw's suggestion these vessels were replaced by armored launches with a hull formed of watertight compartments covered by steel-plate armour to protect the engines, fuel and crew.

'Their design betrays the vices of haste, but they are cheap, safe and afford wonderful practice,' commented Lawrence at the time. 'The financial people refuse the crews extra pay, which we are pressing for – not because we think it dangerous, but because it is damned uncomfortable! Hellish hot, smelly and noisy. They wear ear defenders, crash helmets, gas masks and little else.'

During the Second World War, the renowned Air Sea Rescue launches, which may well have owed much to Lawrence's ingenuity, practical application and designs, were based at the town end of Bridlington Harbour.

Lawrence had his final discharge interview on Monday 25 February 1935, telling his CO that he was planning to go south on his bicycle, visiting friends on the way. The CO's record ends: 'Lawrence – he is an exceptional airman in every respect and his character and general conduct has at all times been very good.'

The following day, Ian Deheer took a couple of photographs of Lawrence on his bicycle, with his right hand touching the brick wall around Bridlington Harbour. These are the last known photographs of Lawrence alive, and the next morning he was seen off by a group of colleagues and friends as he headed south.

'On Tuesday I took my discharge from the RAF, and started southwards by road... My losing the RAF numbs me, so that I have not much feeling to spare for a while. In fact I find myself wishing all the time that my own curtain would fall.'

There are several reports of Lawrence's departure from Bridlington to travel south to visit friends. The next day he cycled as far as Cambridge, where he saw his youngest brother, Arnold, a professor at the university. He then went on to Clouds Hill but could not cope with the reporters hanging around and soon left for London, still cycling: 'Romsey on Sunday night; and London by 4 p.m. Monday: 75 miles that second day! Improving!' (Letter to P. Knowles, 19 March 1935)

T. E. Lawrence, Bridlington Harbour,
26 February 1935. Photograph by Ian Deheer

Under the name T. E. Smith, he toured the southern counties, staying in Youth Hostels. After years of travelling by motorcycle, he was enjoying riding on a bicycle again: 'It's dull work when the wind's against but, in lanes and sheltered places and in calms or before winds, wholly delightful. So quiet: one hears all the country noises. Cheap – very! Not tiring, up to 60-70 miles a day, which is all that I can achieve, with sight seeing.' (Letter to G. Brough, 5 April 1935)

The Fatal Crash – the closing chapter, Sunday 19 May 1935

On 13 May 1935, just eleven weeks after leaving East Yorkshire, Lawrence made the short journey through Bovington Camp to the post office at Wool, 2½ miles away, to send a telegram to Henry Williamson, author of *Tarka the Otter*. Returning to Clouds Hill along Tank Park Road, he came off his motorcycle having swerved to miss two 14-year-old boys on bicycles. He clipped the back of one of the bikes, skidded across the road and was thrown into the air. Lawrence and the boy were both unconscious, with Lawrence bleeding heavily from his nose and the top of his head. Both were taken by army truck to Bovington Military Hospital.

Lawrence sustained a 9-inch fracture of the skull and other serious head injuries, dying in hospital without regaining consciousness. The boy survived.

Although Lawrence had been a civilian for ten weeks, the inquest took place in a small dining room at Bovington Camp, presumably to exclude the public and the prying media. Others believe it was to avoid pertinent questions being asked. Either way, the verdict of 'accidental death' was seen as controversial and, unsurprisingly, conspiracy theories abound.

Corporal Catchpole, who witnessed the accident as he was walking his dog, mentioned the presence of a black car, but was later instructed to change his evidence. It was also alleged that both boys were advised not to include a black car in their submissions. The coroner was unhappy with the evidence but his verdict still stood: 'What caused the deceased to run into the pedal cyclist from the rear we shall never know,' he opined, 'but the evidence would leave me to think that Mr Shaw may well have been travelling at a high speed and possibly lost control of his motor-cycle.'

Corporal Catchpole thought Lawrence had been travelling at 50-60mph. It was revealed that the motorcycle had jammed in second gear, so his actual speed is open to speculation, like so many aspects of the life and death of T. E. Lawrence.

It is believed that Lawrence was replying to a letter received from Henry Williamson, requesting a meeting regarding the unfinished tribute to Williamson's school chum and First World War fighter pilot Victor Maslin Yeates, who had died in December 1934.

'I'll call in anyway on Tuesday unless rainy day,' ended Williamson.

Lawrence's telegram in reply suggests that he welcomed the visit: 'LUNCH TUESDAY WET FINE. COTTAGE ONE MILE NORTH BOVINGTON CAMP'

Williamson was a friend of Sir Oswald Mosley, founder of the British Union of Fascists. Was he asking for a meeting in the hope that Lawrence could be persuaded to join the movement and perhaps meet Hitler? Again, a view open to conspiracy theories, speculation and debate.

Many theories surrounding Lawrence's death have been voiced over the years. Several friends had received letters from Lawrence indicating that he was depressed and some thought he might have committed suicide, but this seems unlikely. Before leaving for the Post Office, he went across to his kindly neighbour, Mrs Knowles, to ask if she needed anything from the shop, as she was going to cook lunch for Williamson the next day – hardly the action of a man considering suicide.

Others argued that foreign agents – French, German or Arab – had 'arranged' the accident, or that Lawrence was killed by British agents before he published a book exposing government secrets. More likely is that the crash was caused by a combination of excessive speed and bad weather – it was pouring with rain at the time. It is accepted that Lawrence found the adrenalin produced by travelling at high speed could snap him out of depression and the roads were usually quiet.

What is undisputed is the evidence of the postmortem, that Lawrence – who was not wearing a crash helmet – died from a 9-inch fracture on the left side of the skull, causing massive bleeding into the brain, plus a fracture of the left eye socket. Ironically, the surgeon who tried to save his life would later become instrumental in promoting the compulsory wearing of crash helmets that ultimately saved thousands of lives.

Lawrence's funeral, held at St Nicholas Church, Moreton, on 21 May 1935, was well attended. General Wavell flew from Aldershot, while three railway coaches brought mourners from London, including Lady Astor, Jonathan Cape, Winston and Mrs Churchill, Mrs Thomas Hardy, Sir Basil Liddell Hart, Augustus John, Air Vice-Marshal Salmond, Mr and Mrs Siegfried Sassoon, and various chargés d' affaires. King George V also sent a message of sympathy to Arnold Lawrence.

'In Lawrence we have lost one of the greatest beings of our time,' Winston Churchill remarked. 'I had hoped to see him quit his retirement and take a commanding part in facing the dangers which now threaten the country.'

After the service, Lawrence was buried at Moreton Cemetery.

Among the 216,000 confidential service records released in 1998 were several regarding Lawrence and his nominations for the Victoria Cross, the Distinguished Service Order, and as Commander of the Order of the Bath. A memorandum also warned that, in any citation for bravery, no mention should be made of his secret mission to the Syrian town of Deraa (where he was to spy on the local Turkish garrison, and where his capture, beating and alleged rape took place).

Lawrence has always divided opinion. One camp believes he showed leadership, initiative, endeavour and diplomacy in uniting the different tribes during the Arab Revolt, and that his post-war efforts to have his political evaluation fully considered were justified; the other sees him as an eccentric opportunist, a maverick who was mentally unstable. Either way, his name lives on, as does the debate over who and what he really was. I have found him one of the most intensely fascinating men I have ever read about, and I certainly envy the Sims family their opportunity to welcome him into their home and to get to know him on a uniquely personal level.

T. E. Lawrence, February 1934. Photograph by Reginald Sims.

SELECT BIBLIOGRAPHY

Richard Aldington, *Lawrence of Arabia: A Biographical Enquiry* (Cassell, 1955)

Michael Asher, *Lawrence: The Uncrowned King of Arabia* (Viking, 1998)

Flora Armitage, *The Desert and the Stars: A Portrait of T. E. Lawrence* (Faber, 1946)

Peter Brett, *T. E. Lawrence* (Book Club Associates 1975)

Malcom Brown, *A Touch of Genius: The Life of T. E. Lawrence* (Dent, 1988)

Robert Graves, *Lawrence and the Arabs* (Cape, 1927)

Basil Liddell Hart, *T. E. Lawrence: In Arabia and After* (Cape, 1948)

Lawrence James, *The Golden Warrior* (Weidenfield & Nicolson, 1990)

Phillip Knightley, *The Secret Lives of Lawrence of Arabia* (Nelson, 1969)

Richard Knowles, *Cats and Landladies' Husbands: T. E. Lawrence in Bridlington* (Fleece, 1995)

A. W. Lawrence, *T. E. Lawrence by His Friends* (Cape, 1954)

T. E. Lawrence, *The Letters of T. E. Lawrence*, ed. David Garnett (Cape, 1938)

T. E. Lawrence, *The Mint* (Cape, 1955)

T. E. Lawrence, *Revolt in the Desert* (Cape, 1927)

T. E. Lawrence, *Seven Pillars of Wisdom* (Cape, 1935)

Paul Marriott and Yvonne Argent, *The Last Days of T. E. Lawrence* (The Alpha Press, 1996)

Anthony Nutting, *Lawrence of Arabia: The Man and the Motive* (Hollis & Carter, 1961)

Reginald Sims, *The Sayings and Doings of T. E. Lawrence*, ed. Leo John de Freitas (Fleece, 1994)

Clare Sydney Smith, *The Golden Reign: The Story of My Friendship with 'Lawrence of Arabia'* (Cassell, 1949)
Desmond Stewart, *T. E. Lawrence* (Harper & Row, 1977)
Henry Williamson, *Genius of Friendship: T. E. Lawrence* (Faber, 1941)